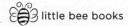 little bee books

An imprint of Bonnier Publishing USA
251 Park Avenue South, New York, NY 10010
Copyright © 2017 by Bonnier Publishing USA
All rights reserved, including the right of reproduction in whole or in part in any form.
LITTLE BEE BOOKS is a trademark of Bonnier Publishing USA, and associated colophon is a trademark of Bonnier Publishing USA.
Manufactured in the United States   LB 0317
First Edition 10 9 8 7 6 5 4 3 2 1

Library of Congress Cataloging-in-Publication Data
Names: Ohlin, Nancy, author. | Larkum, Adam, illustrator.
Title: Great Wall of China / by Nancy Ohlin; illustrated by Adam Larkum.
Description: First edition. | New York, NY: Little Bee Books, 2017.
Series: Blast back! | Includes bibliographical references. | Audience:
Ages 7-10. | Audience: Grades 4-6. | Identifiers: LCCN 2016057765
Subjects: LCSH: Great Wall of China (China)—Juvenile literature.
Classification: LCC DS793.G67 O37 2017 | DDC 951/.156—dc23
LC record available at https://lccn.loc.gov/2016057765

ISBN 978-1-4998-0387-7 (pbk) | ISBN 978-1-4998-0388-4 (hc)

littlebeebooks.com
bonnierpublishingusa.com

THE GREAT WALL OF CHINA

by Nancy Ohlin   illustrated by Adam Larkum

little bee books

CONTENTS

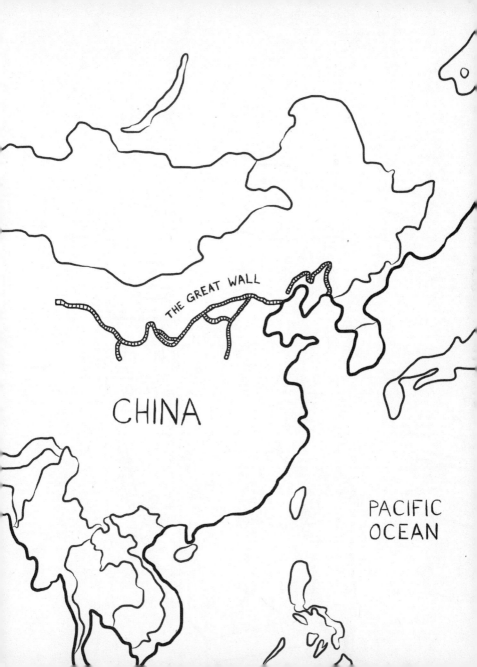

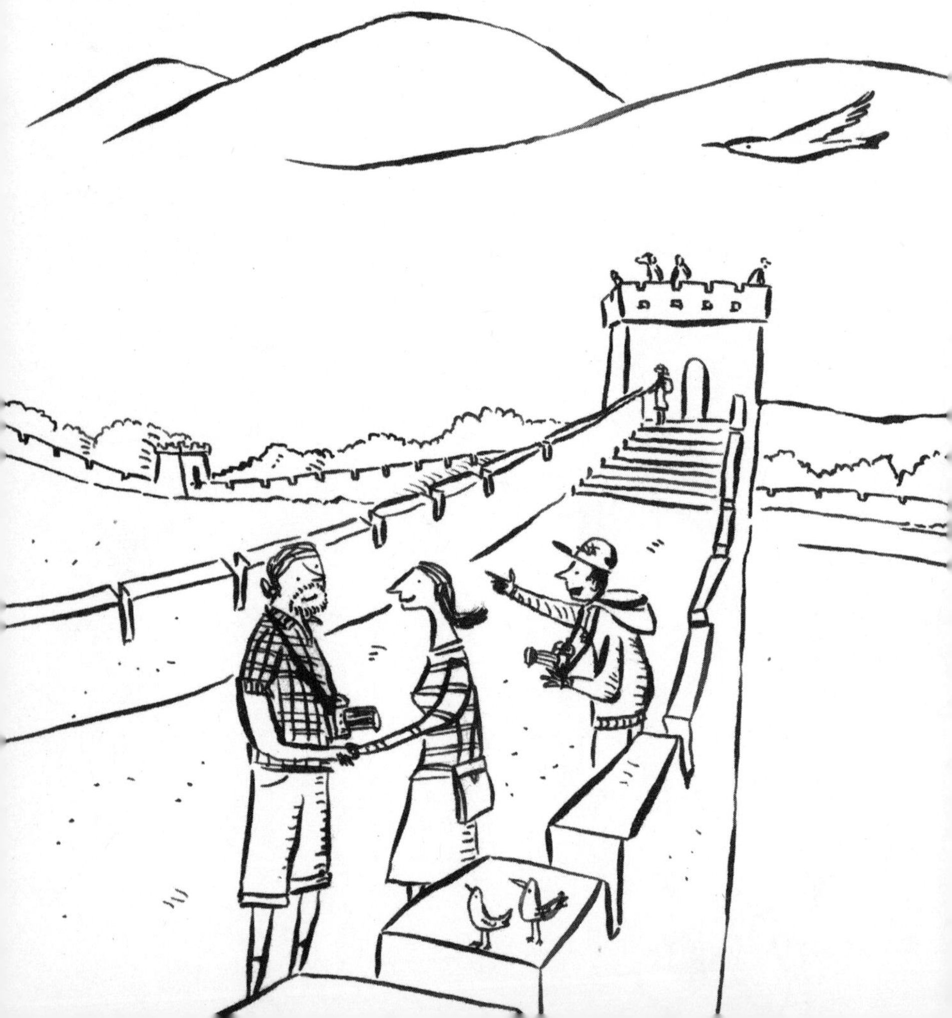

Introduction

Have you ever heard people mention the Great Wall of China and wondered what they were talking about? Why is it "great"? When was it built? What was its original purpose? Does it still exist today?

Let's blast back in time for a little adventure and find out. . . .

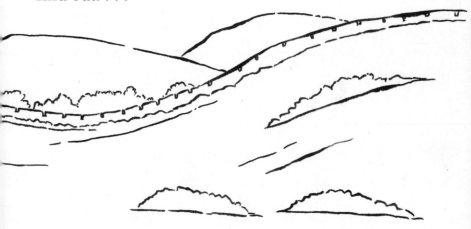

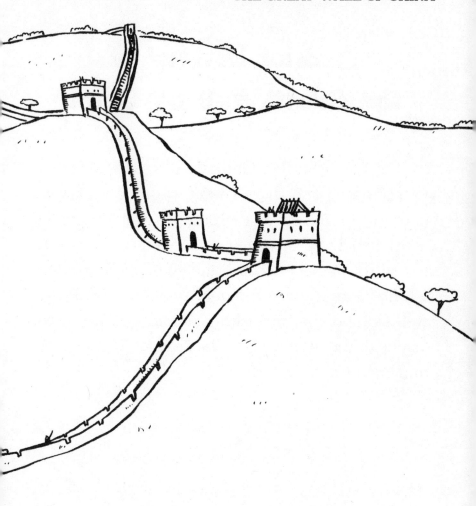

A Brief History of the Great Wall of China

The Great Wall of China is a massive wall that winds through northern China, with the sea at one end and the desert at the other. It was originally constructed to protect against foreign enemies, and to control who could come and go between parts of China. Today, it is a national symbol of China as well as a popular tourist attraction. It is regarded as one of the most spectacular feats of architecture and engineering in history.

THE GREAT WALL OF CHINA

Construction of the Great Wall spanned approximately two thousand years throughout northern China and southern Mongolia. It began as different unconnected walls that were later joined together; more walls were built after that. It included towers for soldiers to stand at guard, gates for people to pass through, castles, forts, beacons, and other structures. A roadway extended along the top. During battles and other conflicts, soldiers could shoot arrows and other weapons through openings in the walls.

The Great Wall has been fixed and added to many times. Some parts of the wall are in ruins or are no longer there.

It's hard to say how long the Great Wall is, exactly, since it was built over such a huge span of time and since some parts of the wall don't exist anymore. Also, not all the wall segments are connected, even to this day.

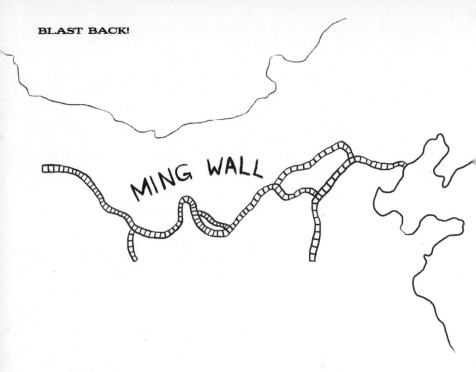

The longest continuous (and best-preserved) part of the Great Wall is around 5,500 miles long. This is the "main wall" (sometimes called the "Ming Wall," after the historical time it was built), which still snakes through the Chinese countryside today. Just to picture how long that is: 5,500 miles is approximately the entire length of the border between Canada and the United States, including Alaska!

The total length of the Great Wall (including unconnected segments) is more like 13,000 miles. (Roughly speaking, 13,000 miles is slightly longer than the distance between the North Pole and the South Pole!)

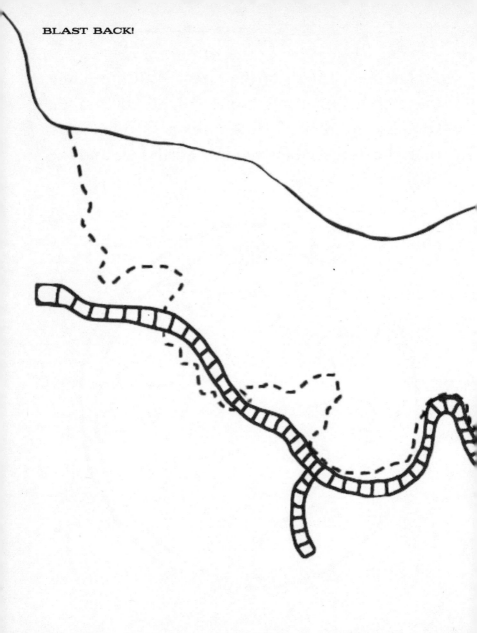

Mongolia

There are sections of the Great Wall in an area that is now called Inner Mongolia. Inner Mongolia is an autonomous (or independent) region in northern China that was established by the Chinese government in 1947.

The sections of the Great Wall in Inner Mongolia were built during a time when the borders between China and the homeland of the Mongolian people were often shifting. Today, Mongolia, formerly called Outer Mongolia, is its own country.

What Is the
Great Wall Made Of?

The Great Wall ranges from around fifteen to twenty-five feet in width and fifteen to thirty feet in height, although there are higher and lower points throughout. Much of the Great Wall is made of dirt, brick, stone, sand, wood, reeds, and other materials that were available in the area at the time. The rest (around a fourth of the wall) is a combination of natural barriers like mountain ridges and rivers, and other types of barriers like moats and ditches.

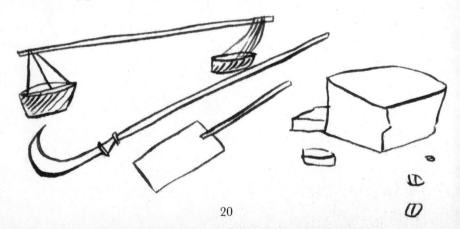

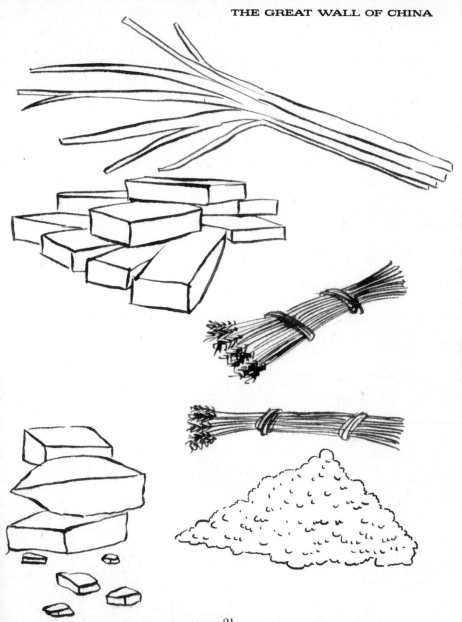

The Great Wall was constructed by human hands and simple tools. One common technique was to pack dirt one thin layer at a time. Each layer was pounded as hard as possible so that the packed dirt was rock-solid and had no air pockets. (This technique was called *hangtu*. "Hang" means "beaten" or "rammed," and "tu" means "earth.")

Bricks were also used in the construction. They were made by filling molds with mud and baking the mud in the hot sun or in ovens. Sections of the wall were paved with stone to create a roadway across the top. Parts of the roadway were wide enough for five men to travel on horse side by side.

Passes and Towers

The Great Wall has a number of passes. A pass is a major stronghold or fortress. The passes in the Great Wall were built with gates, towers, access ramps, and parapets (low protective walls). Passes were used as access points for merchants and other civilians to pass through. They were also used to send out patrols (to survey the area for enemies) and troops (to fight against enemies).

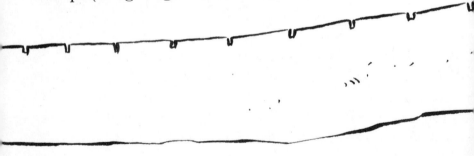

The towers along the wall served several purposes. Soldiers could stand guard at the top and keep watch in case enemies approached. They could also signal others using smoke, fire, lanterns, banners, clappers (two flat sticks that are clapped together to make noise), guns, or other methods. The lower levels of the towers had rooms for the soldiers, stables for their animals, and storage areas. Towers were built at regular intervals, sometimes on hilltops, and rose high above the wall for maximum visibility.

Where Does the Great Wall End?

The western terminus (or end point) of the Great Wall is the Jiayu Pass in the Gansu Province. But what about the eastern terminus?

For a long time, the main wall of the Great Wall was believed to end in the east at the Shanhai Pass in the Hebei Province at the coast of the Bo Hai Sea (which is an arm of the Yellow Sea and also known as the Gulf of Chihli). This meant a total length of around 4,160 miles.

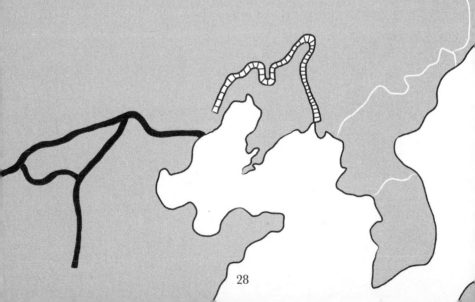

But starting in the 1990s, new sections of the wall were discovered farther east of the Shanhai Pass, in the Liaoning Province. Aerial and satellite surveillance showed that the wall extended continuously through much of the Liaoning Province, went over Hushan (Hu Mountain), and ended near the border between China and North Korea. In 2009, the Chinese government made an announcement about this newly discovered part of the Great Wall. They also updated the length of the main wall to be around 5,500 miles in length.

What Is Pinyin?

Shanhai, *Hushan*, and other Chinese words in this book are pinyin versions of the original words. Chinese words are written in characters and not Roman letters (A, B, C, etc.). Pinyin is a form of "Romanizing" Chinese words, or converting them into the Roman alphabet based on how they sound.

我 wǒ
I; me

岁 suì
years (of age)

吃 chī
to eat

大 dà
big

思 sī
to think

写 xiě
to write

读 dú
to read

马 mǎ
horse

失　算　性　此　必
了　不　们　这　一
时　样　也　和　下
太　该　当　经　妈
间　哪　西　己　候
工　许　东　名　同
思　部　场　嗯　计

China Before the Great Wall

China is one of the world's oldest civilizations, along with Egypt, Mesopotamia, Mesoamerica, and others. There are written records about China that date back to around 1500 BCE. It is believed that Chinese people began to settle, form communities, and farm the land around 2000 BCE.

Over time, small states and kingdoms emerged, each with their own rulers, and these states and kingdoms fought against one another for power and territory. Then dynasties began to control larger and larger territories. (A dynasty is a series of rulers who are part of the same family.)

One of the earliest known dynasties was the Shang dynasty, which took control over part of China around 1700 or 1600 BCE. Around 1050 BCE, the Shang state was taken over by the Zhou state,

and the Shang dynasty was replaced by the Zhou dynasty. The Zhou dynasty remained in power until around 256 BCE.

The Beginnings of the Great Wall

The period from 770 to 476 BCE during the Zhou dynasty was known as the Spring and Autumn Period. During this period, existing and new states continued to vie for territory and power. Around the seventh century BCE, the Chu state started to build the Square Wall, which was to be a permanent fortification for protection against other states and foreign invaders. (A fortification is a defensive wall or other structure.)

The Spring and Autumn Period was followed by the Warring States Period (475–221 BCE). At this point, there were only seven or so states fighting against one another.

During these two periods, many states followed the Chu state's lead and began building their own defensive walls. Some of these walls ran parallel to one another. The Qi state constructed a wall that went all the way to the Yellow Sea. The Zhongshan state built a wall to protect against the Zhao and Qin states. The Wei state built one wall to protect against the Qin state and invaders from the west, and another to protect its capital. The Zhao state built two walls, one of which was for protection against the Wei state. And so on and so on.

These fortifications were the beginnings of the Great Wall.

Confucius

The Spring and Autumn Period was named after a historical account called the *Spring and Autumn Annals*, which is believed to have been written by the Chinese philosopher and teacher Confucius. Confucius is one of the most important, influential, and revered figures in Chinese history, and his ideas are still taught today.

Confucius believed that ordinary people could become extraordinary members of society by constantly improving themselves and striving for goodness. He was also a great believer in education. Before his ideas became widespread, rich Chinese families hired private tutors for their sons. Confucius believed that education should be available to everyone. He also helped to make teaching an actual vocation (job).

A Unified China, a Unified Wall

By the end of the Warring States Period in 221 BCE, one state emerged victorious over the rest: the Qin state. Thus began the Qin dynasty and a unified China.

The young Qin ruler, Zhao Zheng, proclaimed himself emperor of all of China and renamed himself Shihuangdi (First Sovereign Emperor). The Qin dynasty is considered to be the first *imperial* dynasty

of China because it was responsible for a new system whereby all Chinese people had to follow one emperor. ("Imperial" means having to do with an empire, and the ruler of an empire is an emperor.)

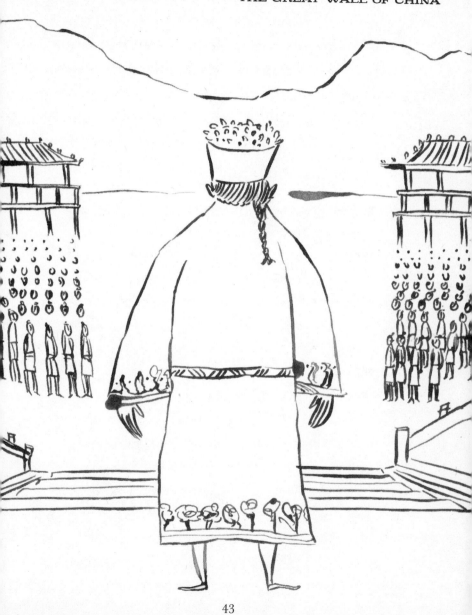

As the new emperor of the newly unified China, Shihuangdi ordered the removal of the fortifications that the states had built between their respective lands. He felt that these defensive walls made it harder for people to travel from place to place within China and for governmental business to be conducted.

Shihuangdi also ordered the fortifications along the northern border of the country (in the Qin, Yan, and Zhao states) to be connected, and for new segments to be built. The resulting wall was called the Wan Li Chang Cheng, or 10,000-Li Long Wall. (A li is a unit of measurement and is equal to about

.31 miles; so ten thousand li is around 3,100 miles, which is the distance between San Francisco and Boston.) Shihuangdi wanted the 10,000-Li Long Wall to help protect against invaders from the north, especially a powerful nomadic group called the Xiongnu. (Nomadic groups move from place to place instead of staying in one location.)

Building the 10,000-Li Long Wall

A general named Meng Tian was put in charge of the 10,000-Li Long Wall project, which started around 214 BCE, and lasted for about a decade. His workforce included hundreds of thousands of convicts (jailed criminals), soldiers, peasants, and others who had been drafted (or forced to sign up) for the job. By some accounts, many of these workers died during the construction process due to difficult and dangerous conditions, and some of their bodies may have been buried under the wall.

The Great Wall from the Han Through the Song Dynasties

The Qin dynasty fell several years after Shihuangdi's death in 210 BCE. Without him, the Great Wall was left largely unprotected and fell into a state of disrepair.

The next dynasty to take over was the Han dynasty (206 BCE to 220 CE). During this period, the Great Wall became a priority again as a means of defense against the nomadic Xiongnu people to the north, who were still a danger. The wall was also used for trade and travel.

For the next millennia and under different dynasties, the Great Wall was repaired and extended many times. There were some periods when the wall was not as much of a priority for defense

because enemies were not such a threat. During the Song dynasty (960–1279), however, the Chinese were under constant threat from the north. At times during this period, work on the Great Wall was impossible because enemies had taken over the surrounding areas.

The Silk Road

The Great Wall helped to protect trade along the Silk Road. The Silk Road was an ancient trade route that connected China with the west. Ideas as well as goods passed back and forth along the four-thousand-mile route. Silk went west from China to the Mediterranean; gold, silver, wools, and other goods went east from the Mediterranean to China. Despite its name (which was coined by a nineteenth-century geographer named Ferdinand von Richthofen), the Silk Road wasn't just one road—it had many branches (including ones to and from India).

The Silk Road started in the east in the Chinese city of Xi'an and followed the Great Wall to the northwest.

The Venetian explorer Marco Polo used the Silk Road to travel to China.

The Great Wall Under Mongolian Rule

From 1271 to 1368, all of China was under the rule of the Mongols, a Central Asian tribal group. This period was known as the Mongol dynasty, or the Yuan dynasty. Genghis Khan, the Mongol ruler and conqueror, started the takeover of China in the early thirteenth century; his grandson Kublai Khan finished the takeover and also became emperor of China. During this time, the Mongols controlled not only China, but other parts of Asia and some parts of Europe, too.

The Mongols didn't really need the Great Wall for defensive purposes. But they did use it for other reasons—for example, to manage trade and other commerce, and to prevent rebellions by citizens.

Kublai Khan

Genghis Khan (whose name means "ruler of all men") died in 1227, and was not able to see his dream of ruling a unified China come true. But Kublai Khan fulfilled his grandfather's dream and became the first Yuan emperor of all of China (as well as the grand khan, or overlord, of the entire Mongol empire).

Kublai Khan was a good leader and was widely accepted by the Chinese people despite being a foreigner and conqueror. Marco Polo lived in Kublai Khan's court for seventeen years. His adventures in China were chronicled in a book based on his stories, *Il milione* (*The Million*).

The Great Wall During the Ming Dynasty

Rebellions and other factors led to the downfall of the Yuan dynasty in 1368, and the Mongols were ousted. This was followed by the Ming dynasty, which was in power from 1368 to 1644.

The Hongzhi emperor, who ruled China during the Ming dynasty between 1487 and 1505, was responsible for most of the Great Wall that stands today (aka the main wall, or the Ming Wall). During this time, the wall was extended and strengthened to prevent another invasion by the Mongols. The wall was divided into north and south lines. The north lines were called the Outer walls, and the south lines were called the Inner walls. There were many strategic passes along the wall, including the Three Inner Passes

and the Three Outer Passes. The Three Inner Passes (the Juyong, Zijing, and Daoma Passes) were built closest to Beijing, the capital of China. The Three Outer Passes (the Piantou, Yanmen, and Ningwu Passes) were farther away, but still important for protecting the capital.

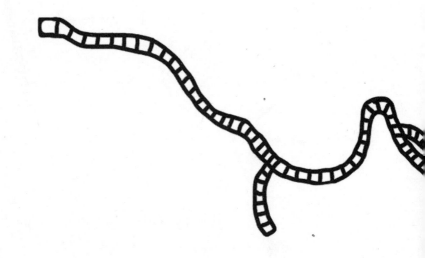

During the Ming dynasty, the wall was improved in other ways. Hundreds of thousands of skilled stonecutters and brick masons were hired to provide building materials. Mules and carts were used to haul the heavy stones from the quarries to the wall. Bricks were baked in cone-shaped ovens called kilns. Drains were constructed to keep rainwater from collecting on the wall and weakening it.

The Ming emperors also wanted the wall to be beautiful and artistic. They demanded details like carved arches over the gates, bricks laid in intricate patterns, and ornately decorated towers.

Gunpowder and the Great Wall

Gunpowder is a mixture that when ignited provides an explosive effect, such as for weapons or mining. The ancient Chinese are generally credited for developing the earliest type of gunpowder, called black powder. They originally used black powder for signals and fireworks.

By the Ming dynasty, both the Chinese and their enemies used gunpowder for weapons like muskets and cannons. The Great Wall had to be strengthened to protect against such weapons. (In its earlier days, the Great Wall had to deal only with simple weapons like spears and arrows.)

Shanhai Pass

The Shanhai Pass, which until recently was thought to be the eastern terminus of the Great Wall, was built in 1381 by a Ming dynasty general named Xu Da. Its Chinese name, Shanhaiguan, means "Pass Between the Mountains and the Sea." It was named so because of its position between the mountains and the Yellow Sea.

A sign above the gate at Shanhai Pass reads: FIRST PASS UNDER HEAVEN. The author of this phrase may have been a medieval-era historian named Xiao Xian. The words refer to the division between China and its enemies to the north.

Part of the Shanhai Pass, called Laolongtou ("Old Dragon's Head"), actually extends out into the sea and resembles a dragon dipping its mouth into the water.

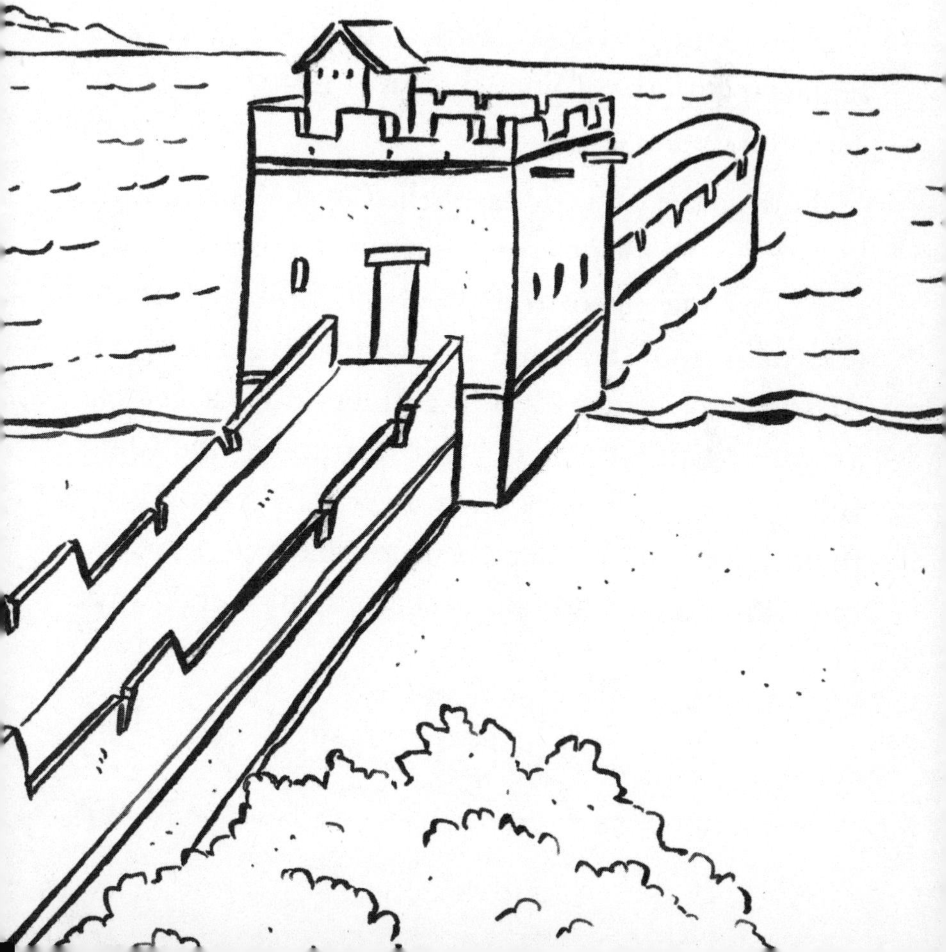

The Great Wall During the Qing Dynasty

The Ming dynasty ended in 1644 and was replaced by the Qing dynasty, also called the Manchu dynasty.

During the Qing dynasty, the Great Wall became less necessary for defensive purposes. For one thing, the Qing managed to expand the Chinese empire and take over the lands of neighboring countries. At the same time, the Qing rulers used a *huairou* (or mollification) policy. With this policy, the Qing rulers tried to mollify their new subjects (or keep them happy) and make them less likely to rebel by respecting their traditions, religions, and other ways of life.

Since the Great Wall was less necessary, it was not repaired often, and much of it fell into ruin over the centuries.

Qing rule lasted until 1911/1912. A countrywide rebellion known as the Chinese Revolution began in October of 1911. At that time, the Qing emperor,

a five-year-old boy named Puyi, was unofficially replaced by a non-imperial leader named Yuan Shikai. Puyi was officially forced to give up his throne in February of 1912. He was the last emperor of China.

The Dynasties of Imperial China

A big part of China's historical timeline is divided into its imperial dynasties. Starting with the Qin dynasty (when China became a unified country), the major dynasties are as follows:

- The Qin Dynasty (221–207 BCE)
- The Han Dynasty (around 206 BCE–220 CE)
- The Six Dynasties (220–589)
- The Sui Dynasty (581–618)
- The Tang Dynasty (618–907)
- The Five Dynasties (907–960)
- The Song Dynasty (960–1279)
- The Mongol Dynasty (early/mid thirteenth century–1368, renamed the Yuan Dynasty in 1271)
- The Ming Dynasty (1368–1644)
- The Qing Dynasty (1644–1911/12)

Gaps and overlaps exist in the timeline because the beginnings and ends of some dynasties were not always clear-cut. Also, there were periods when a number of minor dynasties ruled briefly, one after the other, or when different dynasties ruled different parts of China.

China Today

Imperial China came to an end in 1912, when Qing rule was formally replaced by a republican form of government and a president. (Under a republican form of government, citizens are supposed to be able to choose their leader, or leaders.) The country was renamed the Republic of China.

In 1949 after a long civil war, the Chinese Communist Party took control, and the country was renamed the People's Republic of China. (Under communism, the government divides up money and goods as needed so that everyone is equal.) China is still officially known as the People's Republic of China.

Today, China is the biggest country in the world in terms of population, with more than 1.3 billion people (which is more than one-fifth of all the people in the world). More than 90 percent of its population

is Han (or native Chinese), and there are fifty-five minority groups as well. The official language is Mandarin.

At almost 3.7 million square miles, China is also geographically big. It consists of thirty-four provinces including the Taiwan Province, although whether or not China actually controls it is in dispute. China is bordered by fourteen countries: Afghanistan, Bhutan, India, Kazakhstan, Kyrgyzstan, Laos, Mongolia, Myanmar, Nepal, North Korea, Pakistan, Russia, Tajikistan, and Vietnam. Its capital city is Beijing.

China is still technically a communist country, but this is changing. Now individuals are allowed to own businesses, and there is a growing middle class.

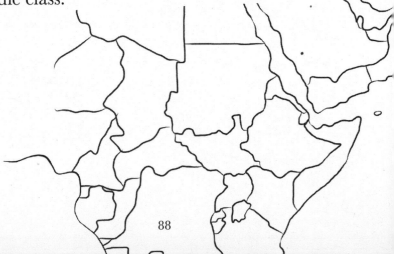

BEIJING

The Great Wall Today

Between 1966 and 1977 was a dark time in Chinese history called the Cultural Revolution. The Communist Party, which had been in charge since 1949, wanted to erase the past and replace it entirely with the party's own ideas and achievements. Valuable artwork was destroyed, as were old and rare books. The Great Wall was impacted as well. Bulldozers and dynamite destroyed hundreds of miles of the wall so that modern roads and buildings could be built there instead.

The West didn't know much about the Great Wall for a long time. Then in 1972, President Richard Nixon became the first U.S. president to visit China. (Its borders had been closed to almost all visitors for two decades.) The communist leader at the time, Chairman Mao Zedong, took President Nixon to the Great Wall. News images of the American president standing at the wall brought worldwide attention to the landmark.

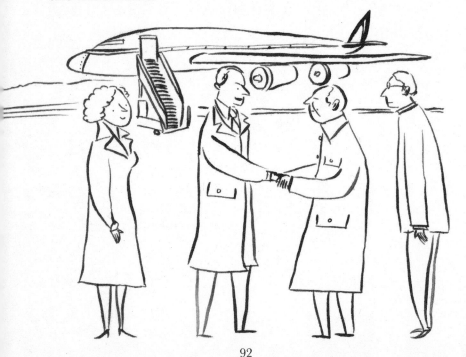

In 1984, a new communist government under a leader named Deng Xiaoping decided that the Great Wall had to be respected and restored, not torn down to make way for new construction.

In 1987, the Great Wall was designated a UNESCO World Heritage site. UNESCO, which stands for the United Nations Educational, Scientific, and Cultural Organization, chose to honor the Great Wall based on its cultural importance.

Today, the Great Wall is a national symbol of China. It is also a major tourist attraction that draws more than ten million visitors each year. The best known (and most visited) section is at Badaling,

which is about forty-three miles northwest of Beijing; thousands of Chinese and foreign tourists visit there daily. The wall at Mutianyu is another popular section.

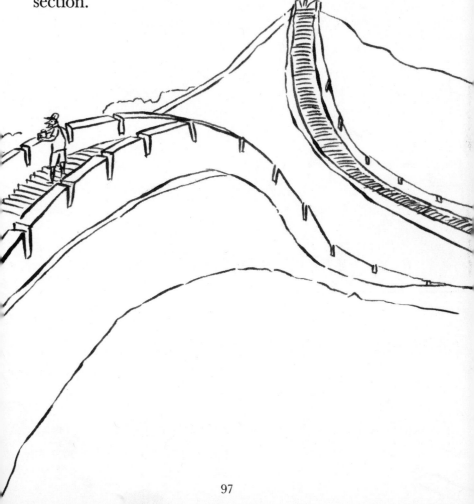

Unfortunately, parts of the Great Wall continue to deteriorate and disappear. Neglect and erosion are major culprits. So is vandalism—people steal bricks, stones, and other artifacts from the wall to keep as

souvenirs or to sell. It is estimated that around a third of the wall has crumbled to dust. Major restoration and preservation efforts are necessary to keep the wall around for future generations.

Are New Parts of the Great Wall Still Being Discovered?

In 2011, an international expedition found what may be two previously unknown segments of the Great Wall—outside of China! With the help of Google Earth, which compiles satellite and aerial images, the team found these wall segments in the Gobi Desert in Mongolia. Originally thought to be a part of a wall called the Wall of Genghis Khan, the researchers theorized that the newly discovered segments were instead parts of the Great Wall built sometime in the eleventh or twelfth century.

Other Famous Border Walls

The Great Wall of China may be the most famous border wall in existence today. But there were other famous border walls throughout history, including:

The Amorite Wall: During the twenty-first century BCE, Sumerian rulers built a defensive wall to keep out a nomadic tribe called the Amorites.

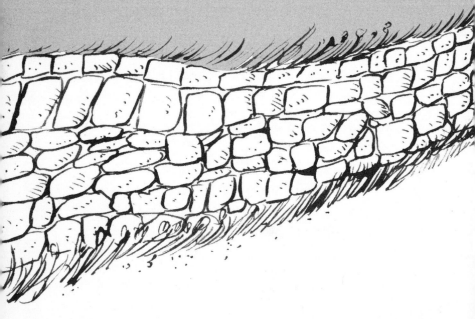

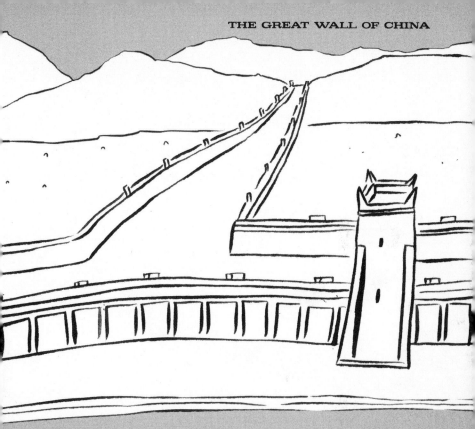

The Long Walls of Athens: Around 461 BCE, Athenians built barrier walls that created a protective triangle around the city, and also connected it to two harbors (which was important for military purposes).

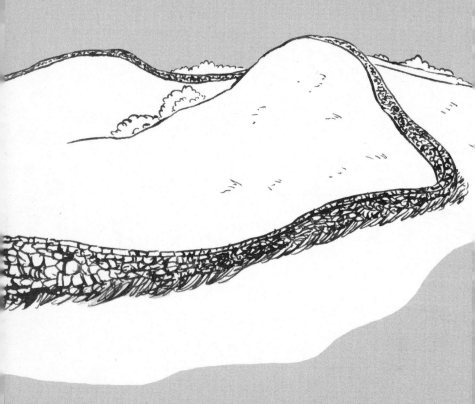

Hadrian's Wall: Around 122 BCE, the Roman emperor Hadrian ordered this stone wall to be built to protect Roman Britain. Many portions still exist in England today.

The Great Wall of Gorgan: Built around the fifth century CE, possibly by the Sasanian Persians, this wall extended 121 miles from the Caspian Sea to the Elburz Mountains (in what is known today as Iran).

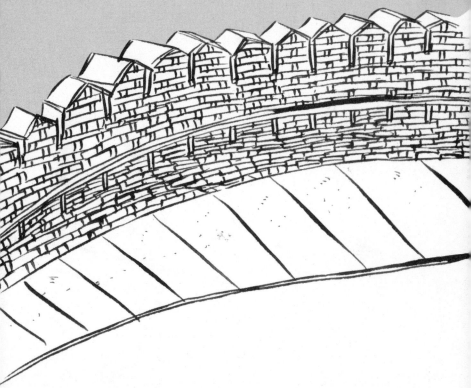

106

The Berlin Wall: This barrier was built in 1961 by East Germany's communist government to separate East Germany from non-communist West Germany, and to keep East Germans from escaping to the other side. Around five thousand East Germans succeeded in crossing the wall to freedom; another five thousand people were captured, and an additional 191 were killed while trying to cross. The East German government finally opened the wall in 1989, and Germany was officially unified in 1990.

Well, it's been a great adventure. Good-bye, Great Wall of China!

Where to next?

Also available:

ANCIENT EGYPT

by Nancy Ohlin
Illustrated by Adam Larkum

ANCIENT GREECE

by Nancy Ohlin
Illustrated by Adam Larkum

THE AMERICAN REVOLUTION

by Nancy Ohlin
Illustrated by Adam Larkum

THE CIVIL WAR

by Nancy Ohlin
Illustrated by Adam Larkum

THE TITANIC

by Nancy Ohlin
Illustrated by Adam Larkum

WORLD WAR II

by Nancy Ohlin
Illustrated by Roger Simo

THE SPACE RACE

by Nancy Ohlin
Illustrated by Roger Simo

THE SALEM WITCH TRIALS

by Nancy Ohlin
Illustrated by Roger Simo

Selected Bibliography

"7 Famous Border Walls" by Evan Andrews, History Online,
http://www.history.com/news/history-lists/7-famous-border-walls

"China's Great Wall is Crumbling in Many Places; Can It Be Saved?" by Anthony Kuhn,
Morning Edition, National Public Radio Online, http://www.npr.org/sections/
parallels/2016/01/27/464421353/chinas-great-wall-is-crumbling-in-many-places
-can-it-be-saved

Encyclopedia Britannica Online, www.britannica.com

Encyclopedia Britannica Kids Online, www.britannica.kids.com

Great Wall of China by Carla Mooney, Rourke Educational Media, 2015

"Great Wall of China," History Online, http://www.history.com/topics/great-wall-of-china

"'Lost' Great Wall of China Segment Found?" by James Owen, National Geographic News
Online, http://news.nationalgeographic.com/news/2012/03/120319-great-wall-of
-china-mongolia-science-lindesay/

Where Is the Great Wall? by Patricia Brennan Demuth, Grosset & Dunlap, 2015

"World's Most Visited Tourist Attractions," Travel & Leisure Online,
http://www.travelandleisure.com/slideshows/worlds-most-visited-tourist-attractions/27

NANCY OHLIN is the author of the YA novels *Always, Forever* and *Beauty* as well as the early chapter book series Greetings from Somewhere under the pseudonym Harper Paris. She lives in Ithaca, New York, with her husband, their two kids, four cats, and assorted animals who happen to show up at their door. Visit her online at nancyohlin.com.

ADAM LARKUM is a freelance illustrator based in the United Kingdom. In his fifteen years of illustrating, he's worked on more than forty books. In addition to his illustration work, he also dabbles in animation and develops characters for television.

112